ideals® EASTER

The lily tells a secret;
The butterfly does too.
The happy bluebird warbles,
"It's true! I know it's true!"

The tulips nod so surely;
The cardinal sings, "Good cheer!"
They also know the secret—
Glad Eastertime is here!
—VELDA BLUMHAGEN

IDEALS PUBLICATIONS

NASHVILLE, TENNESSEE

Blanket

Edna Hill Maples

Snow slips in quietly
Knitting a blanket to cover
Early daffodils.

The First Flowers of Spring

Evalyn Torrant

You golden-petaled flowers
With blossoms like the sun,
You herald spring's approach
And tell us winter's done.
But then a drifting cloud
Conceals the sun from sight,

And snowflakes cover up
Each blossom's little light,
Which saddens us—and yet
Our hearts retain a glow
As you maintain your blooms
Beneath the ice and snow.

Photograph by William H. Johnson

March

William Cullen Bryant

The stormy March is come at last,
With wind, and cloud, and changing skies;
I hear the rushing of the blast,
That through the snowy valley flies.
Ah, passing few are they who speak,
Wild, stormy month! in praise of thee;
Yet, though thy winds are loud and bleak,
Thou art a welcome month to me.
For thou, to northern lands, again
The glad and glorious sun dost bring;
And thou hast joined the gentle train
And wear'st the gentle name of Spring.
And, in thy reign of blast and storm,
Smiles many a long, bright, sunny day,

When the changed winds are soft and warm,
And heaven puts on the blue of May.
Then sing aloud the gushing rills
In joy that they again are free,
And, brightly leaping down the hills,
Renew their journey to the sea.
The year's departing beauty hides
Of wintry storms the sullen threat;
But in thy sternest frown abides
A look of kindly promise yet.
Thou bring'st the hope of those calm skies
And that soft time of sunny showers,
When the wide bloom on earth that lies
Seems of a brighter world than ours.

Spring

Alfred Tennyson

Now fades the last long streak of snow;
Now bourgeons every maze of quick
About the flowering squares, and thick
By ashen roots the violets blow.
Now rings the woodland loud and long,
The distance takes a lovelier hue,
And drowned in yonder living blue
The lark becomes a sightless song.
Now dance the lights on lawn and lea,
The flocks are whiter down the vale,

And milkier every milky sail
On winding stream or distant sea;
Where now the seamew pipes, or dives
In yonder greening gleam, and fly
The happy birds, that change their sky
To build and brood, that live their lives
From land to land; and in my breast
Spring wakens too; and my regret
Becomes an April violet,
And buds and blossoms like the rest.

Photograph by Dennis Frates

Easter

Edwin L. Sabin

The barrier stone has rolled away,
And loud the angels sing;
The Christ comes forth this blessed day
To reign, a deathless King.
For shall we not believe He lives
Through such awakening?
Behold, how God each April gives
The miracle of spring.

Buttercups and Daisies

Mary Howitt

Buttercups and daisies,
Oh, the pretty flowers!
Coming, ere the springtime,
To tell of sunny hours.
While the trees are leafless,
While the fields are bare,
Buttercups and daisies
Spring up everywhere.
Ere the snowdrop peepeth,
Ere the crocus bold,
Ere the early primrose
Opes its paly gold,
Somewhere on a sunny bank
Buttercups are bright;
Somewhere 'mong the
        frozen grass
Peeps the daisy white.
Little hardy flowers,
Like to children poor,
Playing in their sturdy health
By their mother's door:

Purple with the north wind,
Yet alert and bold,
Fearing not, and caring not,
Though they be a-cold.
What to them is weather?
What are stormy showers?
Buttercups and daisies
Are these human flowers!
He who gave them hardship
And a life of care,
Gave them likewise
        hardy strength
And patient hearts to bear.
Welcome, yellow buttercups!
Welcome, daisies white!
Ye are, in my spirit,
Visioned a delight—
Coming ere the springtime,
Of sunny hours to tell,
Speaking to our hearts of Him
Who doeth all things well.

A Moment in a Garden

George Gissing

All about my garden today, the birds are loud. To say that the air is filled with their song gives no idea of the ceaseless piping, whistling, trilling, which at moments ring to heaven in a triumphant unison, a wild accord. Now and then, I notice one of the smaller songsters who seems to strain his throat in a madly joyous endeavor to out-carol all the rest. It is a chorus of praise such as none other of earth's children have the voice or heart to utter. As I listen, I am carried away by glorious rapture; my being melts in the tenderness of an impassioned joy; my eyes are dim with I know not what profound humility.

The Bluebird

Thomas Bailey Aldrich

Hark! 'tis the bluebird's venturous strain
High on the old, fringed elm at the gate:
Sweet-voiced, valiant on the swaying bough,
Alert, elate,
Dodging the fitful spits of snow,
New England's poet laureate
Telling us that spring has come again!

Beneath these fruit-tree boughs that shed
Their snow-white blossoms on my head,
With brightest sunshine round me spread
Of spring's unclouded weather,
In this sequestered nook how sweet
To sit upon my orchard-seat,
And birds and flowers once more to greet,
My last year's friends together.

—William Wordsworth

Roozengaarde display garden, Mt. Vernon, Washington. Photograph by Dennis Frates

The Bluebells of New England

Thomas Bailey Aldrich

The roses are a regal troop,
And modest folk the daisies;
But, Bluebells of New England,
To you I give my praises—

To you, fair phantoms in the sun,
Whom merry spring discovers,
With bluebirds for your laureates,
And honeybees for lovers.

The south-wind breathes, and lo!
   you throng
This rugged land of ours:
I think the pale blue clouds of May
Drop down and turn to flowers!

By cottage doors along the roads
You show your winsome faces;

And, like the specter lady, haunt
The lonely woodland places.

All night your eyes are closed in sleep,
Kept fresh for day's adorning:
Such simple faith as yours can see
God's coming in the morning!

You lead me by your holiness
To pleasant ways of duty;
You set my thoughts to melody,
You fill me with your beauty.

Long may the heavens give you rain,
The sunshine its caresses;
Long may the woman that I love
Entwine you in her tresses!

*Spring is come home with
her world-wandering feet.
—Francis Thompson*

The Resurrection and the Life

Edith Shaw Butler

And now the crocus breaks the sod,
And now the bird gives voice to song
Confirming human faith in God
Beyond the winter season long.
For after sleep there comes this hour
To fill the heart with certainty;
From Earth's dark tomb there sprang
    a flower,
The faith that rose from Calvary.

Easter

Elsie M. Carroll

A dry brown bulb covered with sod;
Rain and sun; a thought of God;
And lo! a flower, waxen white;
A heart of gold; a star of light.

A crawling thing, ugly and slow,
Weaving a shroud. But God must know;
A cocoon bursts; a flutter, a sigh;
The soaring flight of a butterfly.

A lifeless form; a grave, a cross.
Bereaved hearts
Numb with loss.
An Easter dawn;
God's brooding wings;
"The dead still live!"
A glad world sings.

WHITE LILIES *by Josephine Trotter.*
Image © Josephine Trotter/SuperStock

Springtime's Message
Esther Lloyd Dauber

Jack-in-the-Pulpit is preaching today—
Listen to what this wildflower would say:
"Be happy in this blessed time of year,
New life is abounding, for springtime is here.
The sun is caressing all living things.
Come, feel the stir as your pulsing heart sings.
Be happy, rejoice, dispel gloom and fear,
And heed nature's message that Easter is here."

The Gift of Easter
Marjorie Bertram Smith

Now every sound and every scene
Blends with overtones of green—
The mist, the rain, the sense of knowing,
And the root renewed in growing.

With turnings of months,
With circlings of days,
The earth lives again
With flowerings of praise.

Photograph by Nobuaki Sumida/relax/Jupiter Images

Easter

Garnett Ann Schultz

Easter hath her blessing
And Easter hath her charms;
Easter is a precious miss
Soft in springtime's arms.

The time of resurrection
Of life and hope anew—
Easter is a treasured time
That brings a peace to you.

Easter hath real meaning:
God is close at hand,
Offering forgiveness
(He can understand).

Let us sing His praises
On this holy day,
Easter is forever;
Keep it just that way.

Sentiments of Easter

Garnett Ann Schultz

A time for tender sentiments
To strengthen faith and love,
When life shall be more meaningful
With hearts that look above;
A new and bright beginning
When spring is at the dawn,
With winter snow and winter dreams
So quickly here and gone.

Easter is the precious time
When love is born anew,
The time our souls hold springtime
    thoughts
And minds grow bigger too;
'Tis hope and faith and rich belief,
'Tis God so very dear,
When springtime blossoms in our
    hearts
The Easter of the year.

Photograph by Larry Lefever/Grant Heilman Photography, Inc.

Bits & Pieces

Now spring has clad the grove in green,
And strew'd the lea wi' flowers . . .
—*Robert Burns*

Hail! festal Easter, that dost bring
Approach of sweetly smiling spring,
When feather'd songsters through the grove
With beasts confess the power of love,
And brighten all the scene.
—*Samuel Taylor Coleridge*

Winter's latest snowflake is the snowdrop flower,
Yellow crocus kindles the first flame of the spring,
At that time appointed, at that day and hour
When life reawakens and hope in everything.
—*Christina G. Rossetti*

'Twas Easter-Sunday. The full-blossomed trees
Filled all the air with fragrance and with joy.
—*Henry Wadsworth Longfellow*

O chime of sweet Saint Charity,
Peal soon that Easter morn
When Christ for all shall risen be,
And in all hearts newborn!
—*James Russell Lowell*

Now that the winter's gone, the earth hath lost
Her snow-white robes; and now no more the frost
Candies the grass, or casts an icy cream
Upon the silver lake or crystal stream. . . .
—*Thomas Carew*

I think of the garden after the rain,
And hope to my heart comes singing;
At morn the cherry-blooms will be white,
And the Easter bells be ringing!
—*Edna Dean Procter*

The World's Springtime

S. D. Gordon

Out of the east comes new light after the darkness of night. And we call it morning. Out of the Easter morning came a wondrous new light—the light of life—after the darkness of sin's night. And it has been the first gleam of a morning, the morning of a new day, for all men. . . .

Easter comes from the East. The one word gives the other. East means the dawn. The original festival of Easter celebrated the spring, the new dawn of the year, and of the earth's life. It is a happy borrowing of a word from our brothers of the earlier ages. Jesus' rising is an Easter, a dawn, the dawn of day for man and for the earth.

Easter spells out beauty, the rare beauty of new life. Is life ever so sweet and beautiful as when it comes up new and fresh in the spring? The green has a fairer hue, the flower a softer, deeper coloring, the air a new balmy freshness, and the dew a sweeter fragrance. Jesus' rising was the beginning of the world's springtime. But it seems to be a slow spring, late in opening up, . . . held back by some hard frosts and rough winter storms. But the sun is coming nearer all the while. It will be warmer soon. Winter will all go.

When Jesus comes again, the frosts will go. Then comes in fully the world's new spring of life, and then the summer full-fruits. The church is not agreed about when that will be; and some see it a long way off, as a sort of great celebration after great victory. Some of us think He may come in any generation, and His coming will bring the great victory. But all are practically agreed that He is to come. When He comes—nobody knows when—then comes the full-fruits of the harvest of life. His coming means release for us up into the Resurrection life. It means reunion with those who have slipped from our grasp. They will come back when He comes back. They come with Him. A wonderous spring morning that!

"And in the morn those angel faces smile,
Which I have loved long since,
And lost awhile."

And the thought makes the heart beat faster, as it fervently repeats John's Patmos prayer, "Come, Lord Jesus."

When it is a bit dark with you—maybe a good bit, a deep biting bit of dark—cheer up; there's a dawn coming. When it is winter in your life—snowbound, icebound, frozen up and frozen in—pull out the full organ stop of your soul and let the music out, for there's a spring coming. And in its wonder, the winter will be sheer forgot. Jesus' springtime of a new life seems to be about due. It may be in your heart now, in your life, like the first crocus up through the snow. It is to be in all the earth. Let us live with our faces turned toward the rising sun—the risen Son.

Betrayal and Arrest

Luke 22:39–54

And [Jesus] came out, and went, as he was wont, to the mount of Olives; and his disciples also followed him.

And when he was at the place, he said unto them, Pray that ye enter not into temptation.

And he was withdrawn from them about a stone's cast, and kneeled down, and prayed,

Saying, Father, if thou be willing, remove this cup from me: nevertheless not my will, but thine, be done.

And there appeared an angel unto him from heaven, strengthening him.

And being in an agony he prayed more earnestly: and his sweat was as it were great drops of blood falling down to the ground.

And when he rose up from prayer, and was come to his disciples, he found them sleeping for sorrow,

And said unto them, Why sleep ye? rise and pray, lest ye enter into temptation.

And while he yet spake, behold a multitude, and he that was called Judas, one of the twelve, went before them, and drew near unto Jesus to kiss him.

But Jesus said unto him, Judas, betrayest thou the Son of man with a kiss?

When they which were about him saw what would follow, they said unto him, Lord, shall we smite with the sword?

And one of them smote the servant of the high priest, and cut off his right ear.

And Jesus answered and said, Suffer ye thus far. And he touched his ear, and healed him.

Then Jesus said unto the chief priests, and captains of the temple, and the elders, which were come to him, Be ye come out, as against a thief, with swords and staves?

When I was daily with you in the temple, ye stretched forth no hands against me: but this is your hour, and the power of darkness.

Then took they him, and led him, and brought him into the high priest's house.

Son of God, Crucified

Mark 15:24–39

And when they had crucified him, they parted his garments, casting lots upon them, what every man should take.

And it was the third hour, and they crucified him.

And the superscription of his accusation was written over, THE KING OF THE JEWS.

And with him they crucify two thieves; the one on his right hand, and the other on his left.

And the scripture was fulfilled, which saith, And he was numbered with the transgressors.

And they that passed by railed on him, wagging their heads, and saying, Ah, thou that destroyest the temple, and buildest it in three days,

Save thyself, and come down from the cross.

Likewise also the chief priests mocking said among themselves with the scribes, He saved others; himself he cannot save.

Let Christ the King of Israel descend now from the cross, that we may see and believe. And they that were crucified with him reviled him.

And when the sixth hour was come, there was darkness over the whole land until the ninth hour.

And at the ninth hour Jesus cried with a loud voice, saying, Eloi, Eloi, lama sabachthani? which is, being interpreted, My God, my God, why hast thou forsaken me?

And some of them that stood by, when they heard it, said, Behold, he calleth Elias.

And one ran and filled a spunge full of vinegar, and put it on a reed, and gave him to drink, saying, Let alone; let us see whether Elias will come to take him down.

And Jesus cried with a loud voice, and gave up the ghost.

And the veil of the temple was rent in twain from the top to the bottom.

And when the centurion, which stood over against him, saw that he so cried out, and gave up the ghost, he said, Truly this man was the Son of God.

The Gardener at the Sepulchre

John 20:1–18

The first day of the week cometh Mary Magdalene early, when it was yet dark, unto the sepulchre, and seeth the stone taken away from the sepulchre.

Then she runneth, and cometh to Simon Peter, and to the other disciple, whom Jesus loved, and saith unto them, They have taken away the LORD out of the sepulchre, and we know not where they have laid him.

Peter therefore went forth, and that other disciple, and came to the sepulchre.

So they ran both together: and the other disciple did outrun Peter, and came first to the sepulchre.

And he stooping down, and looking in, saw the linen clothes lying; yet went he not in.

Then cometh Simon Peter following him, and went into the sepulchre, and seeth the linen clothes lie,

And the napkin, that was about his head, not lying with the linen clothes, but wrapped together in a place by itself.

Then went in also that other disciple, which came first to the sepulchre, and he saw, and believed.

For as yet they knew not the scripture, that he must rise again from the dead.

Then the disciples went away again unto their own home.

But Mary stood without at the sepulchre weeping: and as she wept, she stooped down, and looked into the sepulchre,

And seeth two angels in white sitting, the one at the head, and the other at the feet, where the body of Jesus had lain.

And they say unto her, Woman, why weepest thou? She saith unto them, Because they have taken away my LORD, and I know not where they have laid him.

And when she had thus said, she turned herself back, and saw Jesus standing, and knew not that it was Jesus.

Jesus saith unto her, Woman, why weepest thou? whom seekest thou? She, supposing him to be the gardener, saith unto him, Sir, if thou have borne him hence, tell me where thou hast laid him, and I will take him away.

Jesus saith unto her, Mary. She turned herself, and saith unto him, Rabboni; which is to say, Master.

Jesus saith unto her, Touch me not; for I am not yet ascended to my Father: but go to my brethren, and say unto them, I ascend unto my Father, and your Father; and to my God, and your God.

Mary Magdalene came and told the disciples that she had seen the LORD, and that he had spoken these things unto her.

Miracles in Gardens

Annie M. Israel

Into the garden the women came,
To the tomb of the One Who'd been crucified,
The One Who had healed the blind and the lame,
And on the cross for all men's sins had died.

But the stone of the tomb had been rolled away;
A shining angel stood there instead,
And the wondering women heard him say,
"He Whom you seek is not here; He is not dead."

Like the miracle in that garden then,
Of the empty tomb and the risen King,
Is the miracle of new life again
In my garden here, that He sends each spring.

For in my garden, too, so windswept and bare,
Each year there's a glad awakening:
Budding trees, singing birds, and blossoms fair—
All the beauty and promise that springtime brings.

Reassurance of God's unfailing love,
Renewal of faith when the world is unkind,
Proof that o'er all things He still reigns above,
His presence, His peace, in my garden I find.

The Beauty and Grace of Easter

Anne Penrod

My garden awakens at Easter
In a rainbow of beautiful hues
With a greater inherent perfection
Than a mortal could ever infuse.

How my soul is refreshed by the pageant
Of this splendid and breathtaking show,
As my garden awakens at Easter,
With a beauty no mortal could sow.

And I'm not in the least discontented
Despite all that a garden can be
For the Savior reminds me that Easter
Was created for mortals like me.

So I praise Father God for His goodness
And the marvelous grace He has shown.
And I thank Him for all that Christ Jesus
Has done for mere mortals alone.

Photograph by Marion Brenner/Botanica/Jupiter Images

THROUGH MY WINDOW

The Gardener's Tale

Pamela Kennedy

*M*arcus stopped his raking when he heard them coming. It was just an hour or so before the Sabbath began, and most good Jews were home making preparations. In the marketplace, Jewish shopkeepers were scurrying about finishing their last bits of business, because no commerce or even foot journeys were allowed for twenty-four hours after sunset. But here came a small group of men and women, carrying something wrapped in white linen. Curious, Marcus wandered a bit closer.

"Lean upon my arm, Mary." A young man tenderly guided a sobbing woman. Two other men, members of the Jewish Sanhedrin, by the look of their robes, carried the linen-wrapped bundle.

"Here is the place," one announced. "I expected to use it for my own burial, but now I lay my Lord here, safe from those who would desecrate Him further."

"It is fitting, Joseph," replied the other, "that we, who could not protect Him during his life, now honor Him in death."

They entered a small cave at the garden's edge, and Marcus crouched beside a tree, watching. Before long, the men and women reappeared, but without the body. Then the men bent their shoulders to a huge stone at the side of the tomb, pushing until it rolled into place with a solid "thunk."

Marcus waited until they left, then tentatively approached the circular stone. It rested in a deep groove, effectively sealing the cavelike tomb. In the twilight breeze, branches nodded, casting long shadows as if waving a somber farewell. Marcus wearily gathered his gardening implements and started for home. A Gentile, he couldn't anticipate the luxury of a day of rest.

Entering the garden the next morning, Marcus expected to find things as he had left them; but instead, a squad of soldiers encamped in front of the tomb. While some guarded the stone, now clearly marked with a Roman seal, others lounged around, napping or playing a game of dice on the hardened earth. They acknowledged Marcus.

Marcus waved his arm, bade them "good morning," then headed towards the far side of the garden. All day he tended overgrown hedges of bougainvillea and, departing at twilight, saluted the soldiers gathered around their campfire.

Early on the third day since witnessing the little funeral procession, as he walked to the garden, Marcus wondered how long Caesar's troops would stand guard over a dead body. Nearing the tomb, he strained for a glimpse of the Romans' red tunics. They were gone. And not only that—the huge stone sealing the tomb was rolled back. Marcus stared, trying to understand what had happened.

Photograph by Robert Cable/Natural Selection/Roberstock

Then he heard the sound of running feet and quickly ducked into the shadows.

A woman hurried to the tomb's entrance, stopped, and peered in. Her shawl blew back revealing her hair hanging in damp strands as she gasped for breath. Then she crept closer. Suddenly, her face was bathed in light emanating from within the cave. A melodious voice echoed across the garden, "Woman, why are you weeping?"

Marcus heard her timid response: "They have taken away my Lord, and I do not know where they have laid Him."

Suddenly, there was a man clothed in a common robe standing a few feet from the grave. Startled, Marcus gasped, and just then the woman turned and saw the man.

"Oh, sir," she asked the stranger, "are you familiar with this garden? If you have carried away my Lord Jesus, would you please tell me where you have laid Him?"

A mixture of compassion and love filled the man's face. He reached out His hand and whispered, "Mary!"

The gardener's mind raced as he stared at the outstretched hand, for there, just above the palm, was the scarlet print of a crucifixion nail.

"Teacher!" the woman knelt before the man, grasping his feet.

"Do not hold on to Me," He gently urged, taking her hands in His own and helping her up. "I have not yet ascended to the Father. But go to My brothers and say to them, 'I am ascending to My Father and your Father, to My God and your God.'"

Mary uttered a cry of joy, gathered her robe around her, and dashed from the garden.

Slowly, Marcus stood, staring in amazement as the man smiled at him, turned, then disappeared into the olive grove. The gardener's heart pounded and his eyes filled with tears. Could it be true? Could this be the man who was executed and buried only three days earlier? Was it possible that life could overcome death? That God could even know one's name? Suddenly Marcus was filled with urgency. Abandoning his tools, he dashed after Mary. He had to discover the truth. If what he had seen and heard was real, there was no end to the possibilities life held. Resurrection was no longer a debate for sages only; it was a reality to be grasped by all men.

Easter

Richard Watson Gilder

When in the starry gloom
They sought the Lord Christ's tomb,
Two angels stood in sight
All dressed in burning white
Who unto the women said:
"Why seek ye the living among the dead?"

His life, His hope, His heart,
With death they had no part;
For this those words of scorn
First heard that holy morn,
When the waiting angels said:
"Why seek ye the living among the dead?"

Who journey the selfsame way—
    O ye of this latter day,
Through morning's twilight gloom
Back to the shadowy tomb—
To you, as to them, was it said:
"Why seek ye the living among the dead?"

The Lord is risen indeed,
He is here for your love, for your need—
Not in the grave, nor the sky,
But here where men live and die;
And true the word that was said:
"Why seek ye the living among the dead?"

Wherever are tears and sighs,
Wherever are children's eyes,
Where man calls man his brother,
And loves as himself another,
Christ lives! The angels said:
"Why seek ye the living among the dead?"

Easter

Humbert Wolfe

Bring flowers to strew His way,
Yea, sing, make holiday;
Bid young lambs leap
And earth laugh after sleep.
For now He cometh forth,
Winter flies to the north—
Folds wings and cries
Amid the bergs and ice.

Yea, Death, great Death is dead,
And Life reigns in his stead;
Cometh the Athlete
New from dead Death's defeat.
Cometh the Wrestler;
But Death, he makes no stir,
Utterly spent and done,
And all his kingdom gone.

Easter Carol

George Newell Lovejoy

O Earth! throughout thy borders
Re-don thy fairest dress;
And everywhere, O Nature!
Throb with new happiness;
Once more to new creation
Awake, and death gainsay,
For death is swallowed up of life,
And Christ is risen today!

Let peals of jubilation
Ring out in all the lands;
With hearts of deep elation
Let sea with sea clasp hands;
Let one supreme *Te Deum*
Roll round the world's highway,
For death is swallowed up of life,
And Christ is risen today!

Easter Dawn

Frances Ridley Havergal

It is too calm to be a dream,
Too gravely sweet, too full of power,
Prayer changed to praise this very hour.
Yes, heard and answered! though it seem
Beyond the hope of yesterday,
Beyond the faith that dared to pray,
Yet not beyond the love that heard,
And not beyond the faithful word
On which each trembling prayer may rest
And win the answer truly best.

Yes, heard and answered! sought and found!
I breathe a golden atmosphere
Of solemn joy, and seem to hear
Within, above, and all around,
The chime of deep cathedral bells,
An early herald peal that tells
A glorious Eastertide begun;
While yet are sparkling in the sun
Large raindrops of the night storm passed,
And days of Lent are gone at last.

Cades Cove, Great Smoky Mountains National Park, Tennessee.
Photograph by Dave Hammaker/Grant Heilman Photography, Inc.

Resurrection

Alice Guerin Crist

All rank on rank the tall
    white lillies stood,
The graceful palms against
    the rose-flushed sky
Showed gemmed with dewdrops,
    and red poppies glowed
Through the rank grass nearby.

All hushed the air was—
    rapt and clear and still;
The earth, late racked with pain,
Felt its insensate form
    with rapture thrill;
And hope was born again.

But in that garden there
    was silence deep;
All nature waited—
    till a ringing cry,
"Rabboni! Master!"
    cleft the dewey air.
And swift the listening sky

Flashed into splendor;
    and the sun leaped up;
And all creation thrilled
    with joy newborn,
Hailing our risen Lord
    with ecstasy
On that first Easter morn.

*Photograph by JTB/drr.net/
JTP Photo Communications, Inc.*

Consider the Lilies

Edward E. Hale

"Consider the lilies, how they grow."
—Matthew 6:28b

They do not grow in any spasm of sudden resolution. They seem to wake up, after long indifference. They seem to rush eagerly to light and air, to burst into blossom as quickly as they can, and then to die. But the truth is that all last year they were collecting and digesting from rain and sunshine and air the material which they use in all this outburst. If the bulb had not done its underground duty then, if all nature in union had not done its work then—if the sun had not shone, the world turned on its axis and flown through space, if the heavens had not clouded and cleared, and raindrops formed and fallen—there would be no lily today. The lily does not have to toil. It does not have to spin. Worlds have moved to and fro that it might blossom, rocks have been ground to powder by glacier and by the tooth of time, soils have been drifted hither and thither as ages have passed by, that the lily might have a place to stand, might have food to digest, might have beauty and fragrance for your delight. What the lily has done or has been in all this infinite movement is this. It has accepted the universe. It has waited for its time, and then has pushed its germ to the sky and its rootlets into the soil. It has not tried to be a law unto itself, or to live and blossom and have a being or some system of its own.

Such hint, at least for our own lives, do we gain when we consider the lilies, how they grow. This is the hint which the Savior meant to give. Eager as He is that you and I shall recognize the present God, shall gain from His presence just the comfort and strength that He did, shall live and move and have our being in Him, He asks us to consider the lilies; for they are trusting God, are obeying the great law of nature in which they have their place and their duty. On the one hand, they do not exaggerate their duty. Therefore, their days are not made wretched by toil. They do their part, but that part is not toil. It is not abject. It is clear enough that the lily enjoys its life with all the heart and soul it has. It does its little part gladly, and from the Infinite Love and Infinite Beauty it accepts the rest. Here is our lesson.

In the great jubilee of springtime, men do not simply celebrate the new life of the world. They are sure to add to that recognition their praise of the beauty and glory of the world. It is that feeling which heaps up your roses on the communion table, and brings to me in the pulpit here the annual glory of my pansies and the sweet, timid blush of my blood-root. . . .

The Power that put the flowers here put me here, because His life is in all His works; and His children, of whom I am one, come closer to Him as they know more and more of His handiwork and enjoy what He enjoys, as they watch the present life in which His creatures live and move and have their being. I say the present life in which they are now growing. God is; His name is I AM. It is not, perhaps, easy to think of Him as acting now, with just the thought and feeling with which the poet says He acted in the beginning, when God said, "Let the earth bring forth grass." But it ought not to be impossible. God now says, "Let the earth bring forth grass." He is saying it at this instant; and, because He is saying it at this instant, the earth is bringing forth grass at this instant. Just the same creation is going forward now which, for convenience of language, we say went forward then, in what, for convenience of language, we call the beginning. Perhaps one feels this present power of a present God a little more vividly when one sees it in an unaccustomed way.

"I Am is Thy memorial still." . . . I wanted to say enough to justify our instinctive passion for flowers, and gardening, and nature, and the woods. I want to do honor to that nerve of the eternal life which runs through it all, and makes its joy part, indeed, and element of the joy of God. This is no poor bit of the pleasure of sense alone. The passion that takes you out-of-doors is not one of the vulgar, selfish, or personal passions . . . Here is the child of God who wants to know what his Father is doing. His own life quickens and warms and grows young as days grow longer and the sun rides higher, and it is in his godly nature and by one of the divine laws that he delights to see how other creatures of God are breaking from their wintry prison. Life seeks life and loves life. In the opening of a catkin of a willow, in the flight of the butterfly, in the chirping of a tree-toad or the sweep of an eagle, my life loves to see how others live, exults in their joy, and so far is partner in their great concern. And this is really what we mean when we say, what I think people generally understand, that a man is apt to be nearer to God when he is out-of-doors than when he is in his home. Literally, this might not be true. But what we are after is the

larger life. We do not want to be limited wholly by things of the flesh, what we shall eat, what we shall drink. What we do need is more of God. It may be some sudden and new hint of Him, it may be the infinite and perpetual lesson of the ocean or of the stars. Always it is life—life larger than a room, life larger than a day. It was when he got outside a room that the first man, in the cool of the day, walked with God. And for us, in these later days, it is that we may walk with God, more and more often, that the Savior bids us "consider the lilies."

The Easter Decorations

Ada Cambridge

O take away your dried and painted garlands!
    The snow-cloth's fallen from each quicken'd brow,
The stone's rolled off the sepulchre of winter,
    And risen leaves and flowers are wanted now.

Send out the little ones, that they may gather
    With their pure hands the firstlings of the birth—
Green-golden tufts and delicate half-blown blossoms,
    Sweet with the fragrance of the Easter earth;

Great primrose bunches, with soft, damp moss clinging
    To their brown fibers, nursed in hazel roots;
And violets from the shady banks and copses;
    And wood-anemones, and white hawthorn shoots;

And tender curling fronds of fern; and grasses
    And crumpled leaves from brink of babbling rills,
With cottage-garden treasures—pale narcissi
    And lilac plumes and yellow daffodils.

Open the doors, and let the Easter sunshine
    Flow warmly in and out, in amber waves,
And let the perfume floating round our altar
    Meet the new perfume from the outer graves.

And let the Easter "Alleluia!" mingle
    With the sweet silver rain-notes of the lark;
Let us all sing together! Lent is over,
    Captivity and winter, death and dark.

This spring as it comes bursts up in bonfires green,

Wild puffing of emerald trees, and flame-filled bushes,

Thorn-blossom lifting in wreaths of smoke between

Where the wood fumes up and the watery, flickering rushes.

—D. H. Lawrence

A Spring Song

Claude Lake

Dark sod pierced by flames of flowers,
    Dead wood freshly quickening,
Bright skies dusked with sudden showers,
    Lit by rainbows on the wing.

Cuckoo calls and young lambs' bleating—
    Nimble arts which coyly bring
Little gusts of tender greeting
    From shy nooks where violets cling.

Half-fledged buds and birds and vernal
    Fields of grass dew-glistening;
Evanescent life's eternal
    Resurrection, bridal Spring!

*Mount Greylock State Reservation,
Massachusetts. Photograph by
William H. Johnson*

Church on Easter
Evelyn Gates Shisler

I went to church on Easter morn
And heard the people sing
The glories of a world reborn
And Christ the risen King;
I saw the congregation bow—
The old, the weak, the strong,
The merry young folk, thoughtful now,
And smiling babes, among—
A blessed privilege 'twas to pray
With friends and neighbors on Easter Day.

Easter Joys
George L. Ehrman

The joys of spring make songbirds sing,
And little children too.
The joys of spring bring gentle rain
And flowers kissed by dew . . .
But, oh, the joy when Easter comes
And all the church choirs sing:
"He lives! He lives! Our Savior lives!
The resurrected King!"

Congregational Church, Greenfield Hill, Connecticut.
Photograph by William H. Johnson

Easter: A Child's-Eye View

Lorraine V. Murray

In the black-and-white photo, my sister and I stand side by side. We are decked out in crisp Easter finery, complete with straw hats.

We are bursting with pride, because in our hands we are cradling something that for us represented the essence of Easter joy: two very fuzzy, tiny baby ducks, which we had named Dippy and Dopey.

Our parents allowed us baby ducks on only one Easter; and we gently looped ribbons around their necks and proudly took them on jaunts around the block. We lovingly cuddled the babies, holding them in our laps on towels.

Some people say ducks—along with rabbits, chicks, and eggs—are beside the point and have nothing to do with the deeper meaning of Easter, but I disagree.

My sister and I were too young to fully understand the notion of Jesus dying on the cross, being buried in a tomb, and rising three days later. We did believe, however, that something wonderful had happened; and we could detect signs of this amazing event mirrored in nature.

Even though we lived in Miami, we noticed little revelations of spring: the appearance of newborn lizards on the patio and some fancy blossoms sprouting on the palm trees. And, like children everywhere, we knew that this day called Easter was celebrated by special customs handed down to us from our parents and their parents before them.

One joyous ritual, of course, was the coloring of eggs, which we dipped ever so carefully into the dyes, and then *ooh-ed* and *aah-ed* when we saw that something as simple as an egg could be transformed into something downright gorgeous.

Many years later I discovered that in Christian tradition, the egg can represent the tomb, out of which the risen Christ emerged. But my sister and I did not discuss symbols. Instead, we debated the best way to create polka dots and stripes.

Flowers were also part of our family's Easter tradition. Each year my dad went out on Holy Saturday and returned with a huge pot of fragrant Easter lilies for my mom. No one discussed the deeper meaning of the lilies, but on some level, we had an inkling that their whiteness bespoke purity and their emergence from the still earth hinted at rebirth. But most of all, when we saw our mom's face, we knew the lilies were about joy.

By Easter Sunday, my sister and I were giddy with anticipation. Soon our Lenten abstinence from sweets would be over, and soon we would welcome the tradition that was dearest to our hearts— the luscious sweet in our baskets.

I later discovered that the tradition of Easter baskets dated back to the days when people would carry their first crops to church for a blessing. But my sister and I didn't know a shred of the history;

all we knew was that Sunday morning we engaged in a mad dash to find our baskets, and then lovingly unearth the jewel-like jelly beans and other goodies from the artificial grass.

There followed an equally mad dash to get dressed, get in the car, and arrive at church on time. There the family sat in the crowded pews, with the alleluias ringing forth like shock waves and the incense mingling with the ladies' perfume.

How hard it was for the kids to concentrate. For one thing, our crinolines were scratchy, and the hats a bit too tight. Also, the thought of the Easter candy waiting at home was almost too much to bear.

We had fasted before Communion, but as soon as we got home, my sister and I were allowed to tear into the succulent wonders waiting in our baskets. To this day, I find it impossible to eat the ear off a chocolate rabbit without breaking into a huge smile.

After polishing off a few rabbits, we joined our parents for our traditional Easter breakfast, which consisted of Neapolitan spinach and ricotta pies baked by our mom the day before.

The photos show the crowd that gathered for this feast: my parents; my sister; me; Aunt Madeline and Uncle August; plus family friends Anna and Joe, Nicky and Armand and their son, Tommy.

Eventually, the meal was over, and the company went home. Then one day, the Easter lily began to look a little worn around the edges and was planted in the yard. And the ducks, my

parents assured us, would be sent to a farm where they would never, ever, under any circumstances, be consumed as someone's Sunday dinner.

As I grew up, I struggled to grasp the meaning of Christ's Resurrection. I knew it was a story about impossible and wondrous things happening, a story about weeping at the foot of the cross and rejoicing at the empty tomb.

Still, at the heart of the Easter story remains an eternal secret to be unlocked. And perhaps children understand the wonder of Easter better than adults.

They grasp the secret of chocolates and fuzzy ducks and the expression on a mother's face when her beloved gives her flowers, the secret of hidden baskets and crowded pews, and aunts and uncles squeezed around a table for a feast.

At heart, Easter is about a promise that was kept, a love that never dies—and a joyous alleluia that echoes in our souls forever.

This Easter Day

Loise Pinkerton Fritz

The sun has set behind the hills
This Easter Day of daffodils,
Of crocuses and lilies white,
Of tulips with their colors bright.

This Easter Day of ringing bells
Resounding over hill and dell,
Proclaiming that there's life anew
When every winter storm is through.

Twilight shades now touch the air
This Easter Day of springtime flair,
Of egg hunts in the neighbor's yard,
Of birdsong that uplifts the heart,

Of love that permeates the earth
And pulsates into a rebirth.
The sun, though set with radiant light,
Still glows to light this Easter night.

Corbett Hill, Portland, Oregon. Photograph by Steve Terrill

Easter Egg Memories

Author Unknown

Easter was always a happy time at our house. We looked forward to the new outfits that Mama worked hard sewing. Her feet pumped the wide treadle and made the sewing machine hum as she created seams, sashes, and fancy ruffles. Sometimes she sewed late into the night to finish them by Easter.

Although our Easter outfits were pretty, and our Sunday school lesson was extra special that day, the pretty baskets and colorful eggs caught and held my attention.

We lived in a small town within walking distance of the stores. Dad walked to town every Saturday morning and gave Mama's carefully written list to the man at the grocery store. All the groceries were put into boxes, loaded in a pickup, and delivered to our kitchen.

The Saturday before Easter, amid all the usual bags and jars were a dozen white eggs and a package of Easter-egg dye.

My sister and I wanted to dye the eggs right away, but we knew better than to ask. We always dyed them in the afternoon. All we could do was

try to hide our excitement and watch as Mama put the groceries away, including the package of dye with the Easter Bunny on it.

Mama was a saver. She hardly ever threw anything away. On our back porch was a box filled with things we no longer used. When we played house, she let us use things from it. When it came time to dye the eggs, we looked through the box for old dishes to put the dyes in. For each dye tablet, we found a bowl with a crack in it or a cup without a handle.

When the eggs had been boiled and cooled and the old dishes washed, we each got to pick a dye tablet. I always picked the yellow one. Mama poured hot water and a little vinegar over each one. As the tablet fizzed; it created a cupful of bright-colored water. Lowering the eggs into the cups, we watched them turn from everyday white into special colors.

We wrote Happy Easter in crayon on some of the eggs before we dyed them. The last white egg was saved for our brother. He poured all the dyes together in a big bowl.

When he raised his egg out of the dye, it was an ugly shade of gray with dark speckles. We always tried to talk him into putting his egg in the bottom of the basket, but he insisted on laying it on top of all the others so everyone would notice it.

Photograph by Plainpicture/Jupiter Images

Another Easter celebration I remember was when my friend and I visited her grandmother. She was a sweet little woman who lived all alone in a big old house. I loved to listen to the stories she told us. One was about dying eggs when she was a girl. There was no easy way to dye eggs back then, but her mother knew how to make colored eggs without dye tablets.

She saved her chickens' white eggs and boiled them. When she was through cooking her fresh spring greens, she soaked some of the eggs in the water. They came out a beautiful shade of green. She used beet juice to stain eggs pink, and the water from cooking onion skins was used to stain yellow ones.

Because food was hard to come by, she never wanted to waste it. The eggs were colored, hidden, and eaten all on the same day.

The tradition of hiding and hunting colored Easter eggs is a lasting one. Whether they're stained, dyed, plastic, or candy, all Easter eggs make bright, sweet memories.

Family ~ Recipes

Fancy Deviled Eggs

6 hard-boiled eggs, peeled
2 tablespoons extra-virgin olive oil
1 tablespoon mayonnaise
1½ teaspoons Dijon mustard
2 tablespoons minced celery
4 teaspoons chopped fresh tarragon
1 tablespoon minced drained capers
2 teaspoons minced shallot
 Salt and pepper
 Sliced celery

Cut eggs in half lengthwise. Transfer yolks to small bowl and mash with fork. Mix in oil, mayonnaise, and mustard. Stir in minced celery, tarragon, capers, and shallot. Season to taste with salt and pepper.

Spoon yolk mixture into whites. Garnish each with celery slice. (Can be made 4 hours ahead. Cover loosely and refrigerate.) Makes 12 egg halves.

Egg Salad

7 hard-boiled eggs, peeled
⅓ cup mayonnaise
1 tablespoon Dijon mustard
¾ cup chopped celery
½ cup thinly sliced green onions
¼ cup chopped sweet pickles
 (such as sweet gherkins)
3 tablespoons finely chopped sweet
 onion (such as Vidalia or Maui)
1 teaspoon chopped fresh tarragon
 Salt and pepper

Cut eggs in half lengthwise. Remove yolks from 3 eggs and reserve for another use. Cut remaining egg yolks and all whites into ½-inch pieces.

In medium bowl, whisk together mayonnaise and mustard. Fold in eggs, celery, green onions, pickles, sweet onion, and tarragon. Season to taste with salt and pepper. (Can be made 6 hours ahead. Cover and refrigerate.) Makes 4 servings.

Layered Egg Sandwiches

2 tablespoons mayonnaise	1 bunch of watercress,
2 tablespoons sour cream	washed and dried
1 tablespoon Dijon mustard	Olive oil
6 hard-boiled eggs, roughly chopped	Lemon juice
12 cherry tomatoes, chopped	Kosher salt
3 tablespoons finely chopped fresh chives	12 slices brioche bread
Salt and pepper	

In a medium bowl, mix mayonnaise, sour cream, and mustard. Fold in eggs, tomatoes, and chives. Season with salt and pepper to taste. Set aside.

Remove watercress stems. In a large bowl, toss watercress with a drop or two of olive oil and a splash of lemon juice. Season to taste with kosher salt.

Spread ¼ of the watercress on one slice of brioche. Layer on another slice of brioche and spread with ¼ of the egg salad. Top with third slice of brioche. Cut off the crusts and slice in half. Repeat with remaining brioche slices. Makes 8 half-sandwiches.

Escarole Soup

2 large garlic cloves, minced	1 head (about 1 pound) of escarole,
2 tablespoons olive oil	washed well and cut into
1 cup chopped onion	½-inch-wide strips
12 cups chicken broth (preferably low-salt)	Salt and pepper
½ teaspoon dried oregano, crumbled	3 hard-boiled eggs,
½ cup tiny pasta shapes,	sliced thin lengthwise
such as egg flakes or pastina	1 cup coarsely grated Parmesan

In a large pot over low heat, cook garlic in the oil, stirring until pale golden. Add onion; cook until onion is softened, stirring constantly. Add broth and oregano. Bring the mixture to a boil. Add pasta and simmer 5 minutes. Add escarole; season with salt and pepper to taste. Simmer 5 minutes more. Serve immediately, topped with egg slices and sprinkled with Parmesan. Makes 8 servings (3 quarts).

Easter Magic

Ruth H. Underhill

There's a special Easter magic
That happens every year;
Just the time the children
Await for Easter cheer.

You can see it in the colors
Of the eggs so bright and gay
That are hidden round the big backyards
This happy Easter Day.

You can see it in the bonnets
Of sparkling flowers and lace
Worn over golden, silky curls
And a precious, beaming face.

You can see it on a rugged cross
Where Jesus died in pain,
For the tomb, it could not hold Him—
He's alive! He rose again!

Children at Easter

Ethel Hollandsworth Bailey

Children love Easter baskets
With their yellows, greens, and blues,
And the candy and the chocolate
And perhaps a toy or two;
And the Easter shoes all shiny,
The new suits and dresses gay,
They are like the lovely flowers seen
Blooming Easter Day.

They magnify the meaning
Of Easter Day—they show
The bright hope of the future
In their happy childhood glow.
It's right and dear and holy,
Their happiness and glee,
For Jesus said, "As ye do for them,
So ye also do for Me."

Happy Easter

Mona K. Guldswog

Here's a basket of Easter eggs for you,
Colored with loving care:
Pink and yellow . . . green and blue . . .
Yours to hold and yours to share.
For pink glows with happiness;
Yellow with fun;
Green, sweet joy;
Blue, dreams begun!
And tucked here and there
Are bright, sunny days
Filled with laughter and love
And friends always!

Easter Memories

Kate Marchbanks

*W*hen I think of Easter, pastel colors always come to mind.

It could be because of the daffodils, tulips, and lilacs that bloom in the spring; or it could be the colored eggs and candy that are part of the celebration. Maybe my memory is of the matching, pastel-colored dresses that my sister and I wore to church on Easter when we were young.

My most memorable Easters were the ones we spent at my grandparents' farm. For several years, my family went there for Easter weekend, and we had our celebration with Grandma and Grandpa.

I remember waking up Easter morning and finding a candy-filled basket next to the bed. Then my sister and I got up and went outside to hunt for eggs, which my grandparents had helped Mom and Dad hide. Mom said that she thought Grandma and Grandpa enjoyed the hunt as much as we did.

After the egg hunt, we had breakfast. The part I looked forward to most was the bunny-shaped pancakes that Grandma made. They just seemed to taste better than regular pancakes.

Then we were off to church, where we enjoyed meeting Grandma and Grandpa's friends and taking part in the Easter service. For dinner, Grandma made bunny rolls and ham.

I was always sad when it was time to go home, but I felt a little better when I remembered the baskets of candy that we could eat along the way.

These traditions signaled the arrival of spring and new beginnings.

Photograph by William H. Johnson

Featured Poet

On Easter

Eileen Spinelli

Fresh-cut meadow scents the dawn.
Yesterday's mistakes are gone.
Winter gray gives way to green.
April is the go-between.
Robins sing in tender trees—
Sweet the song across the breeze.
Laughing children circle-dance.
Grownups get a second chance.
Lilies bloom where weeds once grew.
Christ is risen . . .

    all is new.

GRANDMA'S TREASURES *by Diane Phalen.*
Image from Diane Phalen Watercolors

A Spring Day

E. B. White

There is a stanza in Robert Frost's poem "Two Tramps in Mud Time" that describes an April moment when air and sky have a vernal feeling, but suddenly a cloud crosses the path of the sun and a bitter little wind finds you out, and you're back in the middle of March. Everyone who has lived in the country knows that sort of moment—the promise of warmth, the raised hope, the ruthless rebuff.

There is another sort of day that needs celebrating in song—the day of days when spring at last holds up her face to be kissed, deliberate and unabashed. On that day, no wind blows either in the hills or in the mind, no chill finds the bone. It is a day that can come only in a northern climate, where there has been a long background of frigidity, a long deficiency of sun.

We've just been through this magical moment—which was more than a moment and was a whole morning—and it lodges in memory like some old romance, with the same subtlety of tone, the same enrichment of the blood, and the enchantment and the mirth and the indescribable warmth. Even before breakfast, I felt that the moment was at hand; for when I went out to the barn to investigate twins, I let the kitchen door stay open, lazily, instead of closing it behind me. This was a sign. The lambs had nursed, and the ewe was lying quiet. One lamb had settled itself on the mother's back and was a perfect miniature of the old one—they reminded me of a teapot we have, whose knob is a tiny replica of the pot itself. The barn seemed warmer and sweeter than usual; but it was early in the day, and the hint of springburst was still only a hint, a suggestion, a nudge. The full impact wasn't felt until the sun had climbed higher. Then came, one after another, the many small caresses that added up to the total embrace of warmth and life—a laziness and contentment in the behavior of animals and people, a tendency of man and dog to sit down somewhere in the sun. In the driveway, a deep rut that for the past week had held three or four inches of water and that had alternately frozen and thawed, showed clear indications of drying up. On the window ledge in the living room, the bare brown forsythia cuttings suddenly discovered the secret of yellow. The goose, instead of coming off her nest and joining her loud compainions, settled down on her eleven eggs, pulled some feathers from her breast, and resigned herself to the twenty-eight-day grind. When I went back through the kitchen I noticed that the air that had come in was not like an invader but like a friend who had stopped by for a visit.

The sun was warm but the wind was chill.
You know how it is with an April day
When the sun is out and the wind is still,
You're one month on in the middle of May.
But if you so much as dare to speak,
A cloud comes over the sunlit arch,
A wind comes off a frozen peak,
And you're two months back in the middle of March.
—Robert Frost, from "Two Tramps in Mud-Time"

Photograph by Peter Dean/Grant Heilman Photography, Inc.

Easter Happiness

Minnie Klemme

May Easter find the bluebird
Winging back to you,
Bringing sunny weather
And heaven's skies of blue.

May Christ, Who gives us Easter
And gives the bluebird too,
Bring you His choicest springtime
And bless your life anew.

ISBN-13: 978-0-8249-1317-5

Published by Ideals Publications, a Guideposts Company
535 Metroplex Drive, Suite 250, Nashville, Tennessee 37211
www.idealsbooks.com

Publisher, Peggy Schaefer
Editor, Melinda Rathjen
Copy Editor, Kaye Dacus
Designer, Marisa Jackson
Permissions, Lori Archer

Cover: Photograph by Grant Heilman Photography, Inc.
Inside front cover: Image from Ideals Publications
Inside back cover: Image from Ideals Publications

ACKNOWLEDGMENTS:

CAPPER'S. "Easter Eggs Bring Back Happy Memories" from *CAPPER'S* magazine, March 19, 2002. Used by permission of Ogden Publications Inc. CRIST, ALICE GUERIN. "Resurrection" from *Eucharist Lilies*, by Alice Guerin Crist. Published by Pellegrini & Co., 1928. Used by permission of the author's estate. FROST, ROBERT. An excerpt from "Two Tramps in Mud-Time" from *The Poetry of Robert Frost*, edited by Edward Connery Lathem. Copyright © 1969 by Henry Holt and Company, copyright © 1936 by Robert Frost, © 1964 by Lesley Frost Ballantine. Reprinted by permission of Henry Holt and Company, LLC. GORDON, S. D. "The World's Springtime," an excerpt from "Day Dawn—A Quiet Talk on Easter," first published in *The Congregationalist*. Used by permission of *The Congregationalist*, www.congregationalist.org. MARCHBANKS, KATE. "Easter Memories" originally titled "A Letter from Kate" from *CAPPER'S* magazine, March 19, 2002. Used by permission of Ogden Publications Inc. MURRAY, LORRAINE V. "Easter: A Child's-Eye View" from *AMERICA* magazine, March 28, 2005. Used by permission. WHITE, E. B. "A Spring Day," an excerpt from "Spring," from *One Man's Meat*. Text copyright © 1941 by E. B. White. Copyright renewed. Reprinted by permission of Tilbury House, Publishers, Gardiner, Maine. OUR SINCERE THANKS to the following authors or their heirs, some of whom we may have been unable to locate: Ethel Hollandsworth Bailey, Velda Blumhagen, Edith Shaw Butler, Elsie C. Carroll, Esther Lloyd Dauber, George L. Ehrman, Loise Pinkerton Fritz, Mona K. Guldswog, Annie M. Israel, Pamela Kennedy, Minnie Klemme, Edna Hill Maples, Louise Lewin Matthews, Anne Penrod, Garnett Ann Schultz, Evelyn Gates Shisler, Marjorie Bertram Smith, Eileen Spinelli, Evalyn Torrant, Ruth H. Underhill, Humbert Wolfe. Every effort has been made to establish ownership and use of each selection in this book. If contacted, the publisher will be pleased to rectify any inadvertent errors or omissions in subsequent reprints.